ON THE TEAM

BASKETBALL

By James Wyatt

Gareth Stevens
Publishing

Please visit our website, www.garethstevens.com. For a free color catalog of all our high-quality books, call toll free 1-800-542-2595 or fax 1-877-542-2596.

Library of Congress Cataloging-in-Publication Data

Wyatt, James, 1982-
Basketball / James Wyatt.
    p. cm. — (On the team)
Includes index.
ISBN 978-1-4339-6438-1 (pbk.)
ISBN 978-1-4339-6439-8 (6-pack)
ISBN 978-1-4339-6436-7 (library binding)
1. Basketball—Juvenile literature. I. Title.
GV885.1.W93 2012
796.323—dc23

                          2011020271

First Edition

Published in 2012 by
Gareth Stevens Publishing
111 East 14th Street, Suite 349
New York, NY 10003

Designer: Michael J. Flynn
Editor: Greg Roza

Photo credits: Cover, p. 1 Thomas Northcut/Riser/Getty Images; pp. 5, 17, 18, 20, 21 Shutterstock.com; p. 6 Chicago History Museum/Archive Photos/Getty Images; p. 10 Jeff Kaufman/Taxi/Getty Images; pp. 13, 14 iStockphoto.com.

Printed in the United States of America

CPSIA compliance information: Batch #CW12GS: For further information contact Gareth Stevens, New York, New York at 1-800-542-2595.

Contents

Words in the glossary appear in **bold** type the first time they are used in the text.

Basketball is a team sport enjoyed by people of all ages. It's also a great way to get exercise and stay healthy.

Although it was first played in the United States, people all over the world love playing basketball today. With **hoops** set up across the country—from school gyms to city playgrounds—it's a sport just about anyone can play. All you need is a basketball and your friends. You can even practice "shooting hoops" by yourself.

THE COACH'S CORNER

Basketball games begin with a tip-off. The referee throws the ball into the air. One player from each team jumps and tries to tip it to a teammate.

You don't need a whole team to play basketball. Many people like to play "one on one."

This basketball game was played in Evanston, Illinois, in 1905.

6

The History of Basketball

Basketball was invented in 1891 by a Canadian teacher working in the United States. James Naismith wanted to create a game that could be played inside during the winter. Basketball spread quickly across the country.

At first, the player with the ball couldn't move. Soon, dribbling—or bouncing the ball with one hand while moving—was added. **Backboards** were added to the baskets. The number of players on each team changed from nine to five. These changes helped create the game we know today.

THE COACH'S CORNER

The first game of basketball was played using a soccer ball and two peach baskets! This is how the sport got its name.

Basketball is played on a court. A court is a rectangle with baskets on the shorter sides. Inside courts have hardwood floors. Some playgrounds have half courts. Others have full courts.

A basketball court has lines painted on it. The end lines and sidelines mark the edges. A smaller rectangle in front of each basket shows where a player stands to make **free throws**. A large half circle in front of each basket shows where **three-point shots** are made.

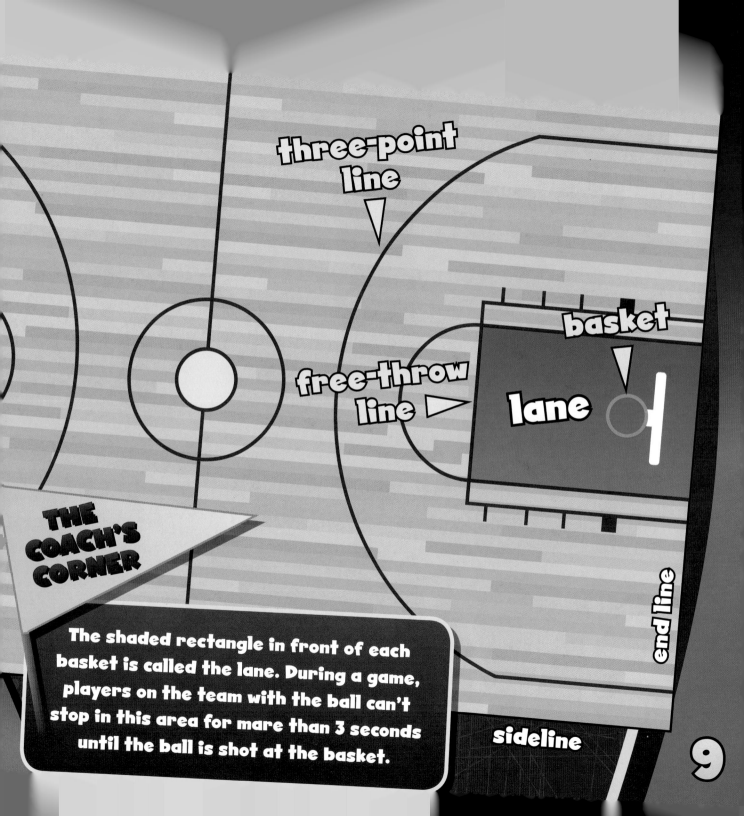

three-point
line
▽

basket
▽

free-throw
line ▷

lane

THE
COACH'S
CORNER

The shaded rectangle in front of each
basket is called the lane. During a game,
players on the team with the ball can't
stop in this area for more than 3 seconds
until the ball is shot at the basket.

end line

sideline

There are different kinds of shots in basketball. This player is trying to make a jump shot.

10

Offense and Defense

Basketball is a fast-paced game. The object is to score the most points by throwing the ball through the top of the basket. Both teams take turns playing offense and defense.

The offense is the team with the ball. They dribble toward the basket, set up plays, and try to score points. The defense tries to stop the offense. They guard players on the other team, block passes, and block shots. Once the defense gets the ball, they become the offense.

THE COACH'S CORNER

Players on both teams try to catch rebounds. A rebound is a shot that bounces off the basket or backboard and comes back into play.

A basketball team usually has two guards on the court. The point guard is often thought of as the leader. Point guards call plays and direct their teammates. They're usually the best dribblers and passers on the team.

The shooting guard is often the best shooter on the team. That player usually takes shots from far away, but must also be good at dribbling past other players for close shots. Shooting guards often play the point guard position as well.

THE COACH'S CORNER

After a basket is made, the ball usually goes to the point guard. That player dribbles down the court behind his teammates and sets up plays.

point
guard

shooting
guard

Point guards must be able to think quickly in order to call the best play.

13

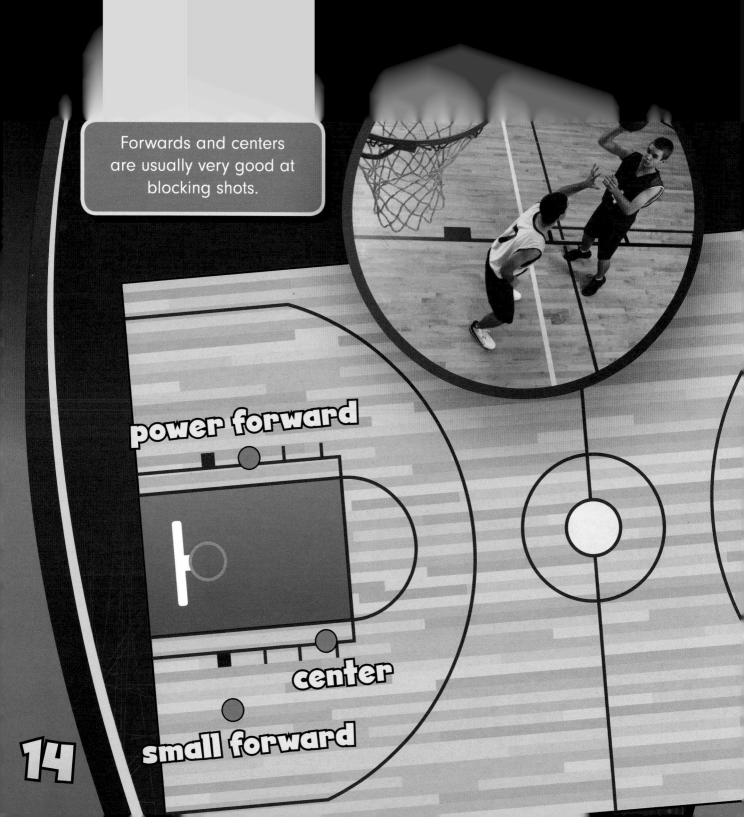

Forwards and centers are usually very good at blocking shots.

power forward

center

small forward

Forwards and Centers

A basketball team has two forwards on the court. Power forwards are tall and strong. They move around the basket while waiting for a pass. They're good rebounders. Small forwards are usually shorter than power forwards, but they play near the end line, too. They're often better outside shooters than power forwards.

Centers are the tallest and strongest players in basketball. They play in the middle of the other players. They're good at getting rebounds and scoring up close.

THE COACH'S CORNER

Outside shooters are players who are good at making shots from farther away from the basket. They're usually good three-point shooters.

Basketball players practice taking shots from different parts of the court. Any shot made inside the three-point line is worth two points. A layup is a shot taken as the player passes under the basket. A jump shot is made during a jump. Three-point shots are long jump shots. They're hard to make, but can increase the score quickly.

Each free throw is worth one point, but referees often give a player more than one free throw at a time.

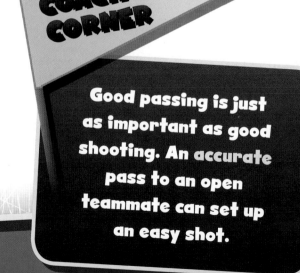

THE COACH'S CORNER

Good passing is just as important as good shooting. An accurate pass to an open teammate can set up an easy shot.

Basketball players learn to use the backboard to bank, or bounce, their shots into the basket.

17

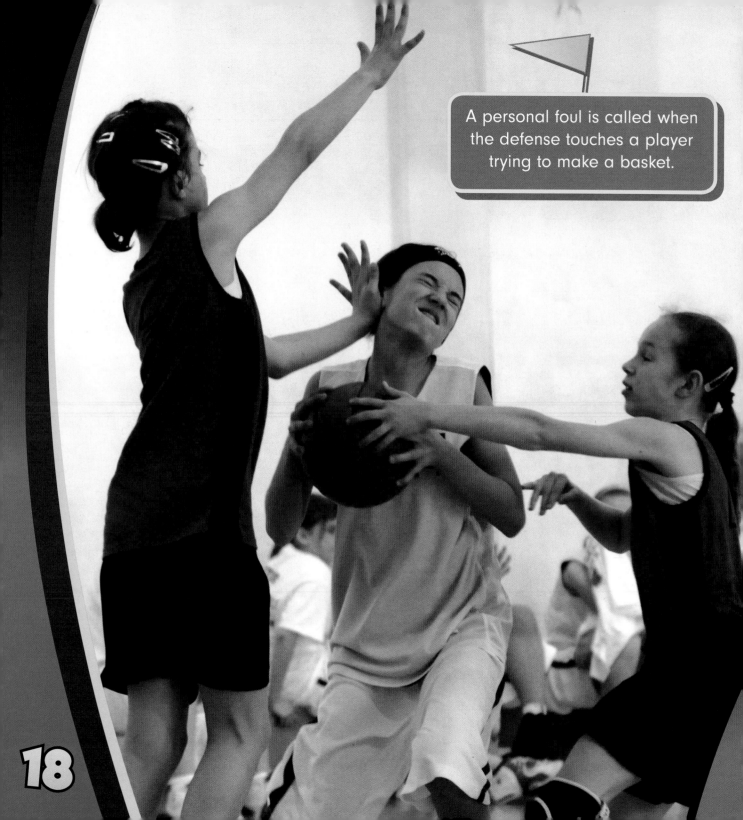

A personal foul is called when the defense touches a player trying to make a basket.

Play by the Rules

Just as in most sports, basketball players must follow the rules. Referees call fouls when a player breaks the rules. Fouls are bad because they give the other team free throws.

Basketball players aren't allowed to stop players on the other team from moving forward. A foul is called when one player runs into or grabs a player on the other team. However, this happens a lot in basketball because the play is so fast. Fighting is also a foul.

THE COACH'S CORNER

If a player moves both feet without dribbling the ball, the referee calls traveling. When this happens, the team loses the ball to the other team.

The Pros

Basketball is a game just about anyone can play. If you practice hard enough, you may even get to play **professional** basketball!

Kids across the world dream of playing pro basketball. The National Basketball Association (NBA) and the Women's National Basketball Association (WNBA) are the two pro basketball leagues in the United States. The players in these leagues have worked hard their entire lives to make it onto a pro team. Keep practicing your basketball skills, and maybe you will, too!

As They Say in Basketball...

bank shot	A shot that bounces off the backboard and into the basket.
bounce pass	A pass where the ball hits the floor before getting to a teammate.
double-team	When two teammates guard a single player on the other team.
field goal	A basket made from anywhere on the court, not including free throws.
hook shot	A shot taken with the arm that is farther from the basket. The arm "hooks" up over the head.
pickup game	A basketball game played among players who just met.
pivot	To spin around while keeping one foot on the floor to avoid being called for traveling.
set a screen	To stand in the way of a defensive player so a teammate can run by them with the ball.
slam dunk	To jump high enough to throw the ball forcefully down into the basket.

Glossary

accurate: free from mistakes

backboard: the flat surface behind a basketball net

free throw: a chance to make a basket without anyone stopping you. This happens after the other team breaks the rules.

hoop: another name for a basketball basket

professional: earning money from an activity that many people do for fun

referee: an official who makes sure players follow the rules

three-point shot: a shot, made from behind a certain line, that is worth three points

For More Information

Books

Hareas, John. *Basketball.* New York, NY: DK Publishing, 2005.

Miller, Amanda. *Let's Talk Basketball.* New York, NY: Children's Press, 2009.

Websites

Basketball
42explore.com/hoops.htm
Learn more about the basic rules of basketball.

NBA Hoop Troop
www.nbahooptroop.com
Watch videos, play games, and find out the latest news about your favorite NBA and WNBA players and teams.

WNBA
www.wnba.com
Keep up to date on the teams and players of the WNBA.

Index

JUL 1 4 2014